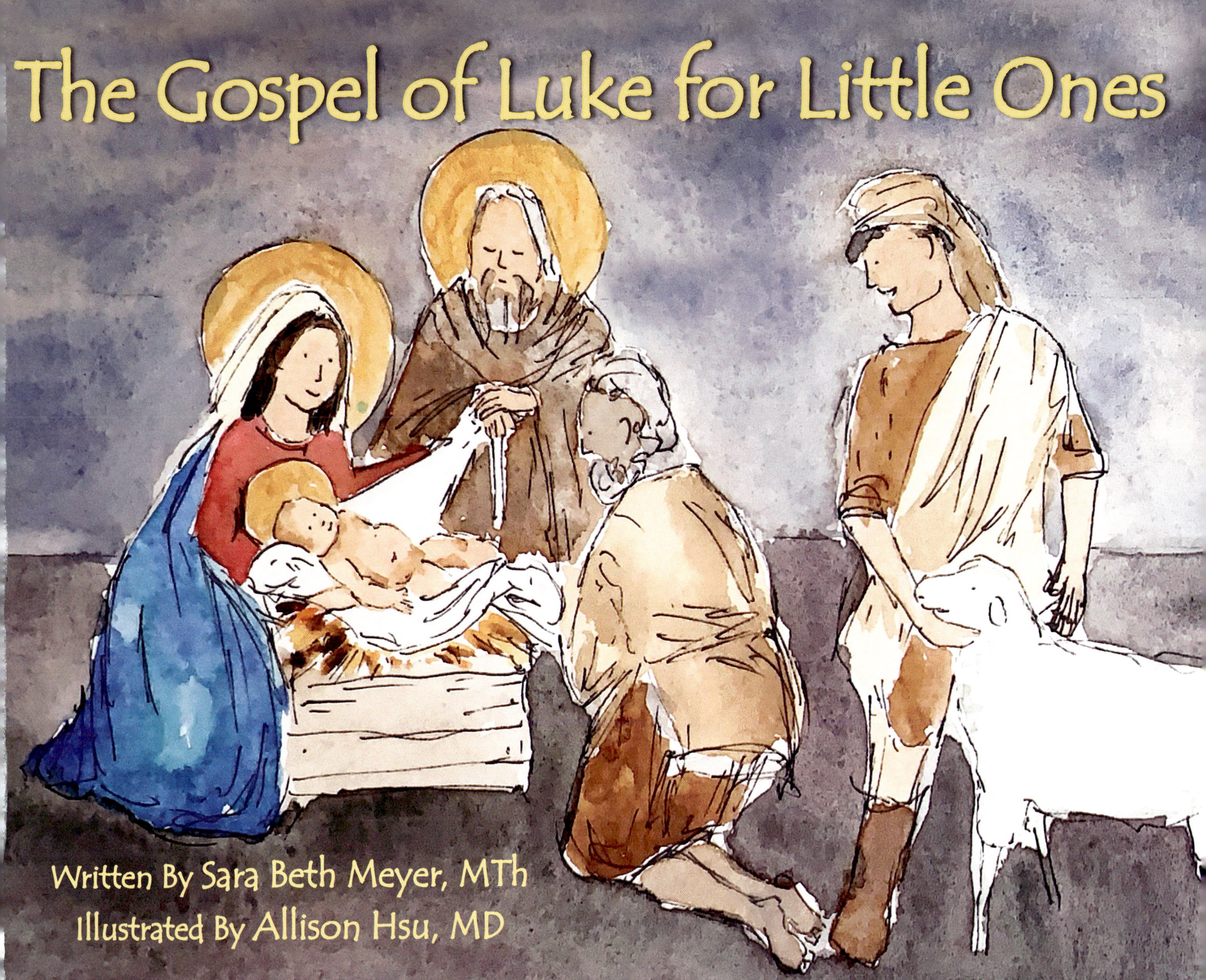
The Gospel of Luke for Little Ones
Written By Sara Beth Meyer, MTh
Illustrated By Allison Hsu, MD

Available from:
Marian Helpers Center
Stockbridge, MA 01263

Prayerline: 1-800-804-3823
Orderline: 1-800-462-7426
Website: ShopMercy.org

ISBN: 978-1-59614-628-0

Imprimi Potest:
Very Rev. Chris Alar, MIC
Provincial Superior
The Blessed Virgin Mary, Mother of Mercy Province
April 8, 2024
Solemnity of the Annunciation of the Lord

Nihil Obstat:
Robert A. Stackpole, STD
Censor Deputatus
April 8, 2024

Printed in the United States of America

Sara Beth: In appreciation for doctors who work mercifully
to extend the healing hand of the Lord,
and for Dr. Allison Hsu,
whose artwork speaks to the spirit.

"For the gifts and the call of God are irrevocable"
(Romans 11:29).

Allison: For all my Little Ones: Sophia, Monica, and
Olivia, Carter, and also Hannah, Kian, Madison, P.J.,
Bridget, Gianna, and Theodore.

About the Authors

Sara Beth Meyer holds a bachelor's degree in education and a master's degree in theology. She enjoys writing articles, books, and songs about faith and family, and is thrilled to collaborate with Allison on *The Gospel of Matthew for Little Ones, The Gospel of Mark for Little Ones*, and *The Gospel of Luke for Little Ones,* especially now that her nine children have begun welcoming Little Ones of their own. She can be found at SaraBethMeyer.com.

Allison Hsu holds a degree in medicine and is an award-winning artist. She is a wife, mother, and illustrator of *The Gospel of Matthew for Little Ones, The Gospel of Mark for Little Ones, The Gospel of Luke for Little Ones,* and the *Little Ones* newsletter. She enjoys using the gift of craftsmanship and sketching the little things of life with great love. She can also be found at SaraBethMeyer.com.

Acknowledgments

We thank everyone who field-tested and gave feedback during the creation phase, the folks at Marian Press who partnered with us in the publication of *The Gospel of Luke for Little Ones*, and the Immaculate Heart of Mary, under whose protection we place this entire project.

An angel came to Zechariah. A miracle was told: *Luke 1*
Elizabeth would bear a son! *But how? They were so old.*
The angel was God's messenger. Gabriel was his name.
He struck the old priest mute; the man's doubting was to blame.

The angel went to Mary next, a virgin girl so pure.
He told her she was favored, and her blessing would endure.
Mary would conceive a child, the Son of the Most High.
"How?" the maiden asked. By the Spirit, he replied.

The angel said Elizabeth was blessed in later years.
Mary rushed to see her. As the greeting reached her ears,
The babe leapt in Elizabeth with joy, and so she knew:
The Lord was with the Virgin. She cried out, "Blessed are you!"

Mary spoke in praises, and she blessed God's Holy Name,
She remained three months with them; then their baby came.
Neighbors said to call him Zechariah, after Dad.
Writing "John" his tongue was freed, and he was so glad.

Mary had to go with Joseph, just before the birth. *Luke 2*
Angels sang out "Glory!" and wished peace to men on earth.
Shepherds went to find the holy Babe and worship too.
They spread the news throughout the land of all that God could do.

After forty days, they went for Jesus' Presentation.
Wise Simeon and Anna both witnessed God's salvation.
Simeon embraced the Babe and blessed our saving Lord,
...then said Mary's tender heart would be pierced by a sword.

One Passover young Jesus stayed, still listening and praying.
His parents left, not knowing that the twelve-year-old was staying.
When they realized He was lost, they searched for three long days.
They found Him with the teachers. When He spoke, all were amazed.

John grew up and went into the desert to baptize. *Luke 3*
He warned against all evil deeds and telling any lies.
Jesus came for Baptism, to show God's way of love.
People heard God's voice and saw the Spirit as a dove.

To the desert, Jesus went to fast for forty days. *Luke 4*
The devil came to tempt Him, in three sneaky ways.
When Jesus would not fall for tricks, the devil finally left.
Then our Lord returned to preach at home in Nazareth.

His neighbors knew Him as a simple man who worked with wood.
They found it strange to hear Him preach. They didn't think He should.
He went to other towns to heal where people did believe.
Crowds began to gather and did not want Him to leave.

Jesus climbed into the boat of tired fishermen. *Luke 5*
They'd worked all night for nothing, but He said to try again.
Their nets all started tearing, as they were so full of fish.
Jesus said to follow Him and "catch" men if they wish.

Simon, Andrew, James, and John all became His friends.
They went with Jesus as He healed the sick and forgave sins.
He called another friend to follow; Levi was his name.
Jesus knew folks made mistakes. He loved them all the same.

Jesus spent the night in prayer, then called another seven. *Luke 6*
He helped the Twelve to share God's love and aim their gaze toward Heaven.
They stayed with Jesus as He taught the people on the plain:
Those who love their enemies are welcome in God's reign.

Jesus healed a servant, from afar when He had heard: *Luke 7*
The master felt unworthy, pleading, "Lord…but say the word."
Soon after, Jesus healed a grieving widow's son who died.
Stories of compassion spread throughout the countryside.

Jesus went to dinner, as a Pharisee's dear guest.
A sinful woman showed she loved our Lord above the rest.
She wept and washed His feet, and then she dried them with her hair.
He said, "Your faith has saved you," shocking all the people there.

Jesus used plain words to show how faith leads to God's glory *Luke 8*
Helping people understand, by telling them a story:
All God's Word is precious seed; our hearts are like the soil.
Bearing good fruit that will last – the only worthwhile toil.

One day, a storm gathered as He slept out on the sea.
His friends all screamed to wake Him, just as fearful as could be.
He calmed the wind and waves, by rebuking with a word.
The twelve men were astonished by what they'd seen and heard.

He sent His friends to all the towns, so they could preach and heal. *Luke 9*
When they returned, He fed 5,000 with one simple meal!
Peter said, "Messiah," but our Lord said not to tell.
Jesus had to suffer. They'd take up their cross as well.

Jesus climbed a mountain with just Peter, James, and John.
They fell asleep and woke amazed by what they gazed upon:
Moses and Elijah spoke with Him, in dazzling white.
A voice called Him "My chosen Son," on that wondrous night.

A man whose son had not been helped, pleaded the next day.
Our Lord rebuked his friends' weak faith, then healed him right away.
Soon the twelve men argued, *which one could be the best?*
Jesus knew their hearts and taught: be least among the rest.

Jesus sent out seventy-two to preach and heal the ill. *Luke 10*
They returned amazed, and yet the people doubted still.
Jesus praised the Father for blessing all the humble:
Little ones can see with faith, while learned men still stumble.

A man heard "love your neighbor," and he wondered who that meant.
Jesus said a man was hurt. Around him, two men went.
A Samaritan stopped on the way. He tended to his needs.
Who acted as a neighbor, in kind and loving deeds?

Jesus went to see some friends: two sisters and a brother.
Mary sat and listened, while Martha served the others.
Upset from working all alone, she asked if it was fair.
He said "the better part" was staying close while He was there.

Jesus taught His followers just how they are to pray: *Luke 11*
Calling God "Our Father" and seeking Him each day.
He said that faith is like a light, brightening the eye.
Good and bad are deep within, not how we look outside.

Jesus said there was a man with harvest beyond measure. *Luke 12*
But he died that very night – so build up lasting treasure.
Be generous! Grow rich in everything you give away.
God loves you, knowing all you need, before you even pray.

Our Lord healed on the Sabbath, which angered several leaders. *Luke 13*
He said they cared for animals with watering and feeders.
Why not care for a woman, who was hurting many years?
The men all left embarrassed when they heard the people's cheers.

At a fancy Sabbath dinner, Jesus saw a sickly man. *Luke 14*
He asked the hosts if He should cure as quickly as He can.
When no one answered, Jesus healed, then explained out loud:
Seek to serve the lowly. God will humble all the proud.

Our Lord came to find the lost. He preached to everyone. *Luke 15*
He showed the value of a missing sheep, a coin, and son:
The young man took his father's wealth, and spent it all in sin.
When he came back so sorry, his father welcomed him.

Jesus told a story of two men: one rich, one needy. *Luke 16*
The rich did not show mercy. He was happy to be greedy.
When dead, the rich man suffered (while the poor enjoyed relief).
He begged to warn his brothers of the everlasting grief.

Ten lepers came for healing, and Jesus cured each one. *Luke 17*
They went away rejoicing, glad to finally have some fun.
One came back to thank our Lord because he felt so fine.
Ten were healed, so Jesus asked, "Where are the other nine?"

He told another story. This time, two men went to pray. *Luke 18*
One man was a Pharisee; one took taxes every day.
One loved his own holiness. One sadly beat his breast.
Only one left justified, as humble prayer is best.

People brought their babies to get Jesus' loving touch.
His friends tried to protect Him, but He loved the kids so much.
He explained that only folks whose hearts are pure like these
Can come into God's Kingdom, then He blessed them and was pleased.

Zacchaeus collected taxes, and he was a little man. *Luke 19*
He climbed a tree to see our Lord out walking through the land.
Jesus saw and said He'd come to visit him that day.
He was thrilled and vowed to give more than he took away.

Our Lord went to Jerusalem to suffer and to die.
People laid their cloaks and worshipped Him as He rode by.
Leaders said to silence them, not to let them shout.
He said if they kept quiet, the stones would all cry out.

Leaders tried to trap our Lord. Each asked a tricky question. *Luke 20*
He knew their hearts and answered all with wisdom beyond mention.
Some said He had spoken well. Their challenges were hard.
Jesus warned His friends that they should always "be on guard."

People wondered when the world would finally end for all. *Luke 21*
Jesus said don't be afraid when nations rise and fall.
When they see signs up in the sky and trouble in the land,
Trust in God and look for Him. "Redemption is at hand."

When it was time for Passover, He shared the bread and cup. *Luke 22*
They became His Body and His Blood when offered up.
His friends could not accept He'd come to suffer and to die.
Jesus said one would betray, and Peter would deny.

He took Peter, James, and John with Him and said to pray.
Meanwhile His friend, Judas, got some money to betray.
The friends kept sleeping until Judas and a mob broke in.
Jesus went with them and knew His Passion would begin.

Jewish leaders questioned Him. They wanted Him to die. *Luke 23*
The Roman leader, Pilate, was confused and wondered why.
He had Jesus whipped and thought all would be satisfied.
The people just kept screaming to see Jesus crucified.

Our Lord took up His Cross, with help from Simon of Cyrene.
People shouted at Him, saying things that were so mean.
He forgave each one of them, and in His last breath
Offered up His Spirit, having saved us with His death.

Some women went to Jesus' tomb that following Sunday. *Luke 24*
They saw that it was empty, with the large stone rolled away.
They rushed to tell His friends, so Peter went and saw it too.
Our Lord began appearing with His Body healed anew.

He visited His friends. He showed His hands and feet and side,
And explained that all had happened as was prophesied.
As He rose into the sky, He blessed all the Eleven
To share God's love with all, for He'll return one day from Heaven.

About The Gospel of Luke for Little Ones

In Luke's Gospel, God humbles the proud and blesses the lowly. In Luke 1, skeptical Zechariah is struck mute while Mary, the simple "handmaid of the Lord," is honored by both Gabriel and Elizabeth. In Luke 18, Jesus explains that the self-righteousness of the Pharisees and His own disciples does not win Heaven, where humble prayers are heard and pure hearts are welcome.

May we have trusting hearts like Mary and all God's Little Ones, to be blessed in our daily lives and for all eternity!

Jesus prayed the Psalms! Ask Jesus to help you learn these verses about humility by heart:

For humble people you save; haughty eyes you bring low. Psalm 18:28

He guides the humble in righteousness and teaches the humble his way. Psalm 25:9

My sacrifice, O God, is a contrite spirit; a contrite humbled heart,
O God, you will not scorn. Psalm 51:19